Cambridge **Discovery Education**™
▶ **INTERACTIVE READERS**

Series editor: Bob Hastings

LIFE IN
MUMBAI

A1⁺

Brian Sargent

CAMBRIDGE
UNIVERSITY PRESS

Discovery
EDUCATION™

CAMBRIDGE
UNIVERSITY PRESS

University Printing House, Cambridge CB2 8BS, United Kingdom

One Liberty Plaza, 20th Floor, New York, NY 10006, USA

477 Williamstown Road, Port Melbourne, VIC 3207, Australia

4843/24, 2nd Floor, Ansari Road, Daryaganj, Delhi – 110002, India

79 Anson Road, #06–04/06, Singapore 079906

Cambridge University Press is part of the University of Cambridge.

It furthers the University's mission by disseminating knowledge in the pursuit of education, learning and research at the highest international levels of excellence.

www.cambridge.org
Information on this title: www.cambridge.org/9781107621671

First published 2014
20 19 18 17 16 15 14 13 12 11 10 9 8 7 6 5

Printed in Dubai by Oriental Press

A catalogue record for this publication is available from the British Library.

Library of Congress Cataloguing in Publication data
Sargent, Brian, 1969–
  Life in Mumbai / Brian Sargent.
    pages cm. -- (Cambridge discovery interactive readers)
  ISBN 978-1-107-62167-1 (pbk. : alk. paper)
  1. Mumbai (India)--Juvenile literature. 2. English language--Textbooks for foreign speakers.
  3. Readers (Elementary) I. Title.

DS486.B7S27 2014
954'.792--dc23

                    2013013701

ISBN 978-1-107-62167-1

Additional resources for this publication at www.cambridge.org

Layout services, art direction, book design, and photo research: Q2ABillSMITH GROUP
Editorial services: Hyphen S.A.
Audio production: CityVox, New York
Video production: Q2ABillSMITH GROUP

Contents

Before You Read:
Get Ready!

India is an exciting country and Mumbai is one of its biggest cities. Read on to learn about life in this busy place.

Words to Know

Complete the sentences with the correct words.

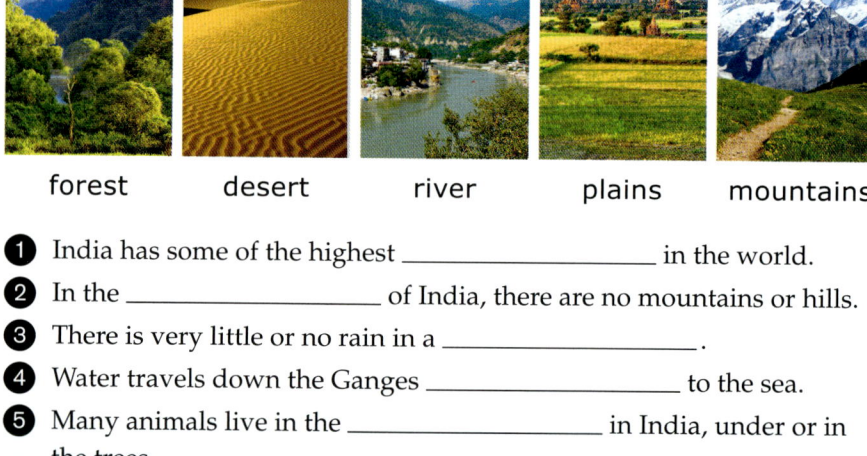

forest   desert   river   plains   mountains

1 India has some of the highest _____ in the world.

2 In the _____ of India, there are no mountains or hills.

3 There is very little or no rain in a _____ .

4 Water travels down the Ganges _____ to the sea.

5 Many animals live in the _____ in India, under or in the trees.

Words to Know

Use the words in the box to complete the blanks.

> east north northeast northwest
> south southeast southwest west

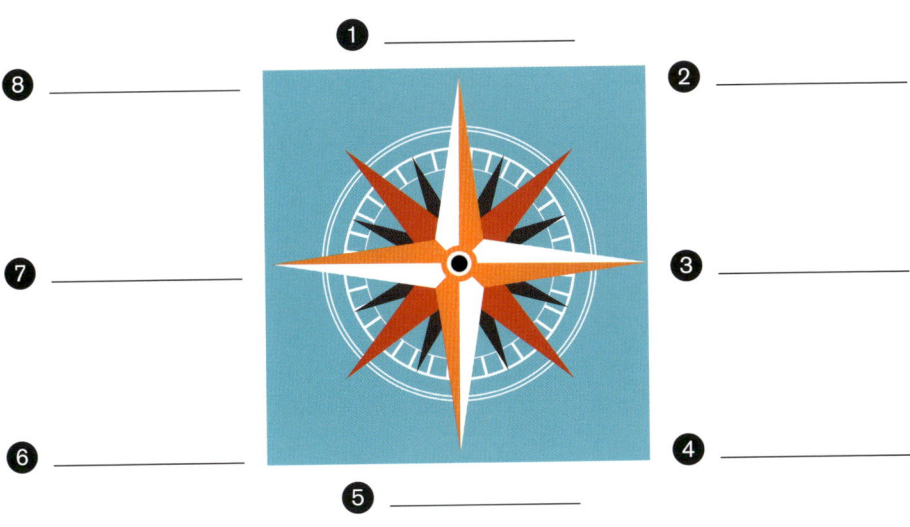

1 _____

8 _____

2 _____

7 _____

3 _____

6 _____

4 _____

5 _____

CHAPTER 1

India at Night

IT'S NIGHT IN INDIA. OVER 1,000,000,000 PEOPLE LIVE IN THIS GREAT COUNTRY. THEY SPEAK MORE THAN 300 DIFFERENT LANGUAGES.

India is a fantastic country with high mountains, big deserts, and many great rivers.

The moon is bright[1] over the Ganges River. In India, this river is called "Mother Ganges." About 3,000 BCE,[2] people began to live by this river. Today, millions[3] of Indians live along it. The Ganges is very important to Hindus, members of the main religion of India. Many Hindus travel a long way to see the Ganges or to wash in its waters.

[1]**bright:** giving strong light
[2]**BCE:** "before Common Era," used for dates before year 1 on our calendars
[3]**million:** the number 1,000,000

It's cold and dark in the great Thar Desert of western India. Life is hard. In May and June, the temperature can be as high as 50° Celsius[4] in the day and as low as 0° Celsius at night. Parts of the desert get only 10 centimeters of rain every year. Not many people live here.

A line of hills or mountains is called a range. The Himalayan mountain range is in the northwest of India. It goes through many other countries, like Pakistan and Nepal. The Himalayas have the highest mountains in the world. Tonight, groups of tourists[5] sleep in tents and wait for the sun to **rise**.

....

[4]**50° Celsius:** fifty degrees Celsius
[5]**tourist:** a person who travels to other places for a holiday

On farms in the central plains of India, the night is very quiet. Many people – about 60 percent – work in agriculture.[6] Soon heavy rains called monsoons are going to come. It doesn't rain often, so the monsoons are very important. Farmers need the monsoons to **grow** rice and other foods, and to grow cotton to make clothes.

The night is noisy in the forests of India. Many different animals live here: elephants, tigers, and rhinoceroses. Some of these animals are in danger,[7] but there are national parks where they can live safely.

[6]**agriculture:** the work of growing plants for food
[7]**in danger:** not safe

Video Quest

Monsoon

Watch this video about the monsoon season. Where does the monsoon travel every year?

It's night in Mumbai, but not everyone is sleeping. People are working. It's a busy city. It's the center[8] of business in India. Over 20 million people live in the Mumbai area. They work in all kinds of jobs. Some of them work in business, or in TV, movies, or music.

[8]**center:** the place where a lot of something is done

CHAPTER 2

Morning in Mumbai

FOR ONE MAN IN MUMBAI, THE DAY ALWAYS BEGINS THE SAME WAY...

Sanjit Gupta wakes up at 5:30 and takes a bath. It's dark, so he lights a **lamp**. He uses *ghee*, a kind of butter, in the lamp. This begins his morning *puja*.[9] Many Hindus begin their day with a morning puja. It's an important part of Hindu life. 80 percent of Indians are Hindu.

[9]**puja (or pooja):** the giving of thanks to Hindu gods or important people

After puja, Sanjit eats *idlis*, small cakes from South India. Sanjit lives in Mumbai now, but he comes from the south of India. When he eats idlis, he thinks about his hometown and his family. He misses[10] them.

Sanjit came to Mumbai to work. He remembers when he was a child. He grew up near farms and hills. In Mumbai he only sees **buildings** and streets.

Sanjit's favorite place in Mumbai is the Dadar flower market. Every morning, farmers bring flowers to the market from their farms near Mumbai. People often buy the flowers in long chains.[11]

[10]**miss:** feel sad when you think about somebody or something you have stopped seeing

[11]**chain:** many things together in one long line

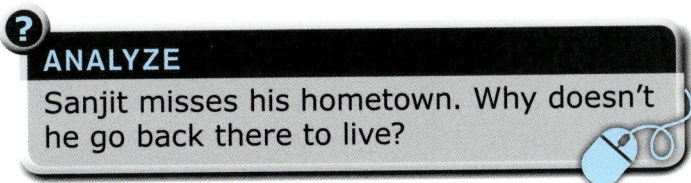

ANALYZE

Sanjit misses his hometown. Why doesn't he go back there to live?

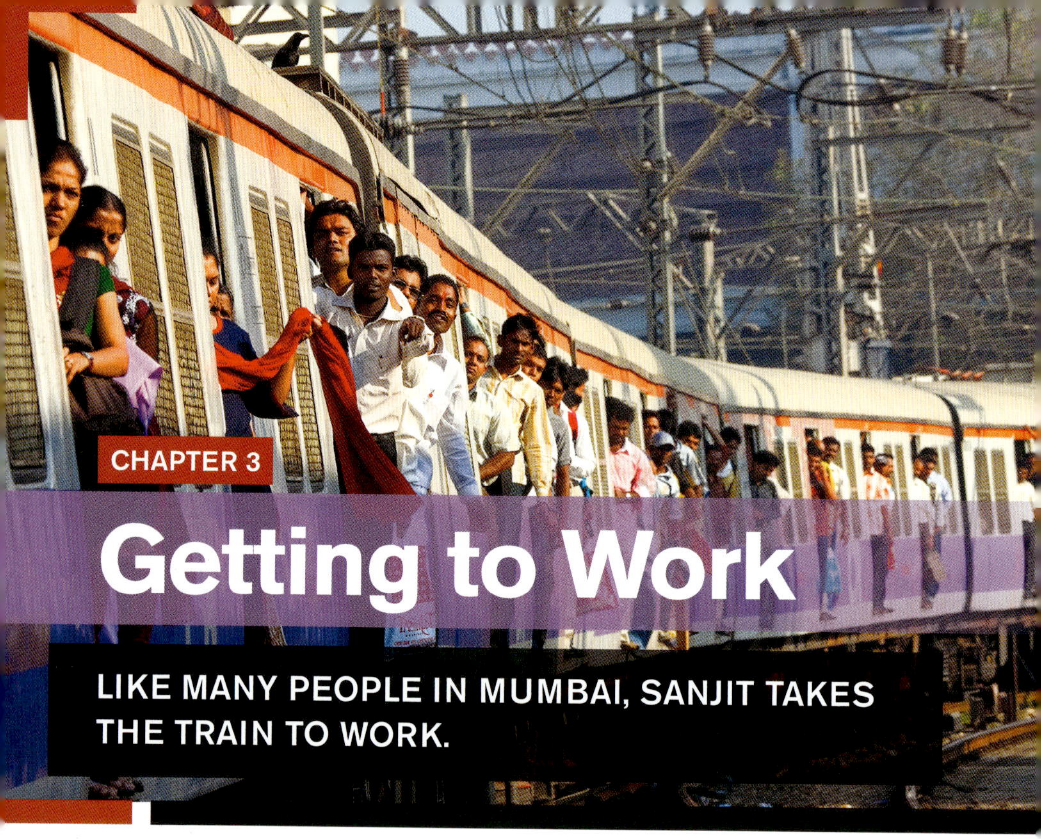

CHAPTER 3

Getting to Work

LIKE MANY PEOPLE IN MUMBAI, SANJIT TAKES THE TRAIN TO WORK.

The trains in Mumbai are famous. They started in 1853, and people in Mumbai call them the *locals*.

The trains are often very old and they are always crowded. Sometimes they are so crowded that the train doors cannot close and people ride on top of the train! Several million people ride the locals every day.

Video Quest

Railways

Watch this video and learn about Mumbai's trains. When are the trains very busy?

There are many buses, taxis, and auto-rickshaws, too. They take people all over the city. The streets are crowded because every year more and more people are coming to Mumbai to live. This is a difficult problem for the city. They must do something, but what?

An Indian auto-rickshaw

Some people think the answer is a different kind of train called a monorail. Monorails often go high above the streets. In 2009, Mumbai started making a monorail. It's going to take many years to finish. People in Mumbai want the monorail today! But for now, they can only ride the crowded trains and buses, and wait.

CHAPTER 4

Working in Mumbai

MANY PEOPLE COME TO MUMBAI FROM OTHER PARTS OF INDIA FOR WORK.

There are many call centers in Mumbai. In a call center, people answer telephone calls. Often call centers answer calls about problems with computers, smart phones, or other kinds of technology.

In the early 2000s, countries like India, the Philippines, and South Africa opened many call centers. In Mumbai, many call centers opened in only a short time. Now some centers are closing. This is because some people in Britain and the US do not like having call centers in other countries.

Sanjit works with computers, but he does not work in a call center. He's a software engineer. A software engineer writes **programs** for computers.

Sanjit works in an office[12] with ten other people. They're working on a game for people to play on the Internet. The game teaches English to children. Sanjit likes computers and helping children learn. Sometimes he wants to leave Mumbai and go back to his hometown. But he knows he cannot find an interesting and fun job there.

....

[12] **office:** a room or building where people work

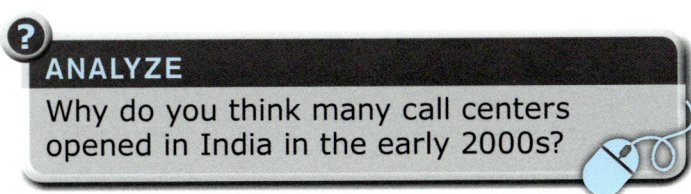

?

ANALYZE

Why do you think many call centers opened in India in the early 2000s?

CHAPTER 5

Home-cooked Lunches for 175,000

IT'S LUNCHTIME, AND SANJIT WANTS HOME-COOKED FOOD. THIS IS NOT A PROBLEM.

Like most people in Mumbai, Sanjit cannot go home for lunch. It's too **far**. Also, Sanjit does not want to ride the crowded locals four times in one day.

Many people in Mumbai want home-cooked lunches. Happily, they can have them, and they are not expensive. Every day, people make and **sell** home-cooked food to workers all over Mumbai. These workers are called *tiffin wallahs* or *dabbawalas*.

Tiffins are small boxes. Inside the tiffins are **traditional** Indian foods, like **curries**, rice, and *phulkas*, an Indian bread.

About 5,000 tiffin wallahs work in Mumbai. They bring over 175,000 tiffins to hungry business people every day. They are fast and very good at their job – 99 percent of the time, the tiffins go to the right places.

Sanjit can buy home-cooked South Indian food from the tiffin wallahs. The lunch is not as good as his mother's food, but it is better than eating at a fast-food restaurant.

Video Quest

Tiffin wallahs

Watch this video to learn about Mumbai's tiffin wallahs. What did the word "tiffin" mean in the past?

CHAPTER 6

An Evening Walk

AFTER WORK, SANJIT DOESN'T WANT TO GO HOME. THE LOCALS ARE TOO CROWDED. HE GOES TO SEE A BOLLYWOOD MOVIE.

Mumbai is home to Bollywood. The name Bollywood comes from Bombay (the old name for Mumbai) and Hollywood. Almost 1,000 movies come out of Bollywood every year. Bollywood movies always have a lot of singing and dancing, often with big groups of people.

Next, Sanjit takes a walk. Monsoon season is coming. It's going to rain every day. Sanjit goes to the Queen's **Necklace**, a three-kilometer road by the Arabian Sea. There are lots of streetlights along this road. At night it looks like a necklace.

At the north end of the road is Chowpatty Beach. Here, people are selling food and children's toys[13] and games. Families have **picnics** on the beach. Children play in the water.

Sanjit buys dinner. He eats it and then walks to the train station. "Mumbai is a busy, crowded city, and I miss my hometown and my family," Sanjit thinks. "But I'm happy to live here."

[13] **toy:** something children play with

?

ANALYZE

A city with 20 million people has many problems. What problem do you feel is the most important? What can the people of Mumbai do to live better?

CHAPTER 7

What Do You Think?

THINK ABOUT IT: YOU WORK IN MUMBAI. WHAT IS YOUR LIFE LIKE?

Mumbai's locals are often very crowded. Usually, only 1,700 people can safely ride in one train. But, before and after work, over 4,500 people ride in one local train in Mumbai. People ride in every part of the train: in open doors, on top of the train. It isn't safe. Thousands[14] of people die every year.

[14]**thousand:** the number 1,000

Think about it: You work in Mumbai. You must get to work every day. The local is fast and cheap, but it is very crowded. Every morning, your train is almost full.[15] What do you do? Do you ride on top? Do you ride in an open door?

Most people on the locals are men, but that is now changing. More women are working in Mumbai. More women are riding the locals, too. In 2009, Mumbai made an important change. They made eight women-only trains. They called the trains the *Ladies' Special*. They run in the morning and in the evening. Many women like the trains.

What do you think about women-only trains? Why do you think Mumbai made them? How do you think the men feel about them?

[15] **full:** has many things or people, and no places for more

After You Read

Read the sentences and choose Ⓐ (True) or Ⓑ (False). If the book does not tell you, choose Ⓒ (Doesn't say).

1 There are no high mountains in India.

- Ⓐ True
- Ⓑ False
- Ⓒ Doesn't say

2 Most Indian people work in agriculture.

- Ⓐ True
- Ⓑ False
- Ⓒ Doesn't say

3 Monsoons happen every month.

- Ⓐ True
- Ⓑ False
- Ⓒ Doesn't say

4 The local trains are very safe.

- Ⓐ True
- Ⓑ False
- Ⓒ Doesn't say

5 Taxis are more expensive than buses.

- Ⓐ True
- Ⓑ False
- Ⓒ Doesn't say

6 The best jobs in Mumbai are at call centers.

- Ⓐ True
- Ⓑ False
- Ⓒ Doesn't say

7 Tiffin wallahs only travel by bike.

  Ⓐ True
  Ⓑ False
  Ⓒ Doesn't say

8 Bollywood is in Delhi.

  Ⓐ True
  Ⓑ False
  Ⓒ Doesn't say

About You

Answer the questions.

1 Where do you live? _____

2 How is it the same as India? _____
_____
_____

3 How is it different from India? _____
_____
_____

Complete the Text

Write one word in each space.

Sanjit's Day

Like many Hindus, Sanjit begins his day with a **1** _____.
Then he takes a **2** _____ called a local to work. Every day a
3 _____ brings him lunch. After work, he takes a
4 _____ on the Queen's Necklace.

Answer Key

Words to Know, page 4

1 mountains **2** plains **3** desert **4** River
5 forest

Words to Know, page 5

1 north **2** northeast **3** east **4** southeast
5 south **6** southwest **7** west **8** northwest

Video Quest, page 8

It travels across India, from the southwest to the northeast.

Analyze, page 11

Suggested Answer: It's hard for Sanjit to find a job he likes there.

Video Quest, page 13

They are busy before and after work.

Analyze, page 15

Answers will vary.

Video Quest, page 17

It's an old English word for "snack."

Analyze, page 19

Answers will vary.

True or False, page 22

1 B **2** A **3** B **4** B **5** C **6** C **7** B **8** B

About You, page 23

Answers will vary.

Complete the Text, page 23

1 puja **2** train **3** tiffin wallah **4** walk